MONEY MOVES

"Mastering Your Personal Finance"

DEDICATION

To all those who have ever felt overwhelmed or intimidated by the world of personal finance, this book is dedicated to you. May it be your guide as you embark on your journey to financial freedom and may it empower you to make money moves that will benefit you and your loved ones for years to come.

Contents

Introduction

Importance of financial literacy

Money is a critical aspect of our lives, and how we manage it can have a significant impact on our financial stability and overall well-being. Unfortunately, many people struggle with personal finances, leading to stress, debt, and a lack of financial security.

Financial literacy is the foundation for making smart money decisions. It is about understanding how money works, making informed decisions about spending and saving, and planning for a secure financial future. Yet, despite its importance, financial literacy is often overlooked, leaving many individuals at a disadvantage when it comes to managing their personal finances.

This is where the book "Money Moves: Mastering Your Personal Finances" comes in. The purpose of this book is to provide you with the knowledge, tools, and strategies to take control of your financial situation, achieve your financial goals, and ultimately, improve your quality of life.

Throughout this book, you will learn how to create a budget, build an emergency fund, manage debt, save, and invest for the future, and protect your wealth. You will also discover how to increase your income, create additional income streams, and maximize employee benefits.

The chapters in this book are designed to provide you with a comprehensive understanding of personal finance, no matter what stage of life you are in. Whether you are just starting out or nearing retirement, this book will give you the knowledge and tools you need to take control of your finances and achieve financial freedom.

By mastering your personal finances, you will have the power to make informed decisions about your money, reduce financial stress, and achieve your financial goals. So, let's get started on this journey together and take the first step towards financial success.

Purpose of the book

The purpose of "Money Moves: Mastering Your Personal Finances" is to provide you with a comprehensive guide to personal finance that will help you take control of your finances and achieve financial freedom. The book is designed to educate, inspire, and empower you to make informed decisions about your money.

By reading this book, you will learn how to create a budget, manage debt, save and invest for the future, protect your wealth, increase your income, and plan for retirement. You will also gain a better understanding of financial concepts such as credit scores, insurance, estate planning, and tax planning.

The goal of this book is not only to help you improve your financial situation but also to help you build the confidence and skills to make sound financial decisions throughout your life. The knowledge and strategies presented in this book will be useful no matter what stage of life you are in, whether you are just starting out or nearing retirement.

Ultimately, the purpose of "Money Moves: Mastering Your Personal Finances" is to provide you with a roadmap to financial success. By following the steps outlined in this book, you will be able to take control of your finances, achieve your financial goals, and live the life you want.

Overview of chapters

Chapter 1: Building a Strong Foundation In this chapter, we will discuss the importance of understanding your financial situation and creating a budget. We will also cover how to build an emergency fund and how to understand your credit scores and reports.

Chapter 2: Managing Debt In this chapter, we will explore different types of debt, strategies for paying off debt, consolidation options, and dealing with collection agencies.

Chapter 3: Saving and Investing In this chapter, we will discuss the importance of saving, types of savings accounts, investing basics, and investing for retirement.

Chapter 4: Making Money Work for You In this chapter, we will cover strategies for increasing income, creating additional income streams, maximizing employee benefits, and starting a side business.

Chapter 5: Protecting Your Wealth In this chapter, we will discuss insurance basics, choosing the right insurance policies, estate planning, and tax planning.

Chapter 6: Planning for the Future In this chapter, we will explore retirement planning, setting financial goals, creating a long-term financial plan, and monitoring and adjusting your plan.

Chapter 7: Conclusion In the final chapter, we will recap the key points covered in the book and encourage you to take action towards improving your financial situation. We will also provide resources for further learning and offer final thoughts on the importance of mastering your personal finances.

Chapter 1: Building a Strong Foundation

In this chapter, we will discuss the importance of understanding your financial situation and creating a budget. We will also cover how to build an emergency fund and how to understand your credit scores and reports.

Understanding Your Financial Situation

Before you can take control of your finances and make effective money moves, you need to understand your current financial situation. This means taking stock of your income, expenses, assets, and liabilities.

1.1. Assessing Your Income

The first step in understanding your financial situation is to determine how much money you have coming in. This includes your salary or wages, any bonuses or commissions, as well as any other sources of income such as rental income, investments, or royalties.

To accurately assess your income, it's important to consider any taxes or deductions that are taken out of your pay checks. If you are self-employed, you will need to keep track of your income and expenses to calculate your net income.

1.2. Identifying Your Expenses

The next step is to determine how much money you are spending each month. This includes your fixed expenses such as rent or mortgage payments, utilities, and car payments, as well as your variable expenses such as groceries, entertainment, and dining out.

To get a complete picture of your expenses, it's important to track your spending for at least a month. You can do this by keeping a detailed record of every purchase you make, either in a notebook or using a budgeting app or spreadsheet.

1.3. Calculating Your Net Worth

Once you have a clear understanding of your income and expenses, you can calculate your net worth. This is the difference between your assets (what you own) and your liabilities (what you owe).

To calculate your net worth, add up the value of your assets (such as your home, car, savings, investments, and personal belongings) and subtract your liabilities (such as your mortgage, credit card debt, and student loans).

Your net worth is an important measure of your financial health and can help you determine whether you are on track to achieve your financial goals.

1.4. Reviewing Your Credit Score and Report

Another important aspect of understanding your financial situation is reviewing your credit score and report. Your credit score is a numerical representation of your creditworthiness, while your credit report provides a detailed history of your borrowing and payment habits.

You can request a free credit report from each of the three major credit reporting agencies (Equifax, Experian, and TransUnion) once a year. Review your credit report carefully to ensure that all the information is accurate and up to date. Your credit score and report can impact your ability to obtain credit, rent an apartment, and even get a job, so it's important to keep them in good standing.

"By understanding your financial situation, you can make informed decisions about your money and develop a plan to achieve your financial goals."

In the following chapters, we will explore strategies for creating a budget, building an emergency fund, paying off debt, and saving for the future.

Creating a Budget

Now that you have a clear understanding of your financial situation, it's time to create a budget. A budget is a spending plan that helps you allocate your income towards your expenses, savings, and financial goals.

Creating a budget can be a daunting task, but it's an essential step towards mastering your personal finances.

2.1. Setting Financial Goals

The first step in creating a budget is to set financial goals. Whether you want to pay off debt, save for a down payment on a house, or invest for retirement, having clear financial goals will help guide your budgeting decisions. Write down your financial goals and attach a dollar amount and a timeline to each one.

2.2. Determining Your Income

The next step is to determine your income. Use your most recent pay stubs or bank statements to calculate your monthly income. If you have irregular income, such as commissions or freelance work, take an average of your income over the past few months.

2.3. Listing Your Expenses

Next, list all of your monthly expenses, including fixed expenses such as rent or mortgage payments, utilities, and car payments, as well as variable expenses such as groceries, entertainment, and dining out. Use your spending records from the previous section to accurately estimate your expenses.

2.4. Categorizing Your Expenses

Once you have listed your expenses, categorize them into essential and non-essential expenses. Essential expenses are those that are necessary for your basic needs, such as housing, food, and transportation. Non-essential expenses are those that are discretionary, such as entertainment, travel, and hobbies.

2.5. Allocating Your Income

Now it's time to allocate your income towards your expenses, savings, and financial goals. Start by deducting your essential expenses from your income. Next, allocate a portion of your income towards your financial goals, such as paying off debt or saving for a down payment on a house. Finally, allocate a portion of your income towards your non-essential expenses.

2.6. Reviewing and Adjusting Your Budget

Once you have created your budget, review it regularly to ensure that you are staying on track. If you find that you are overspending in certain categories, look for ways to reduce your expenses, such as cutting back on eating out or cancelling subscriptions. If you find that you have extra money left over each month, consider allocating it towards your financial goals or savings.

> *"Creating a budget is a key component of mastering your personal finances. By setting financial goals, listing your expenses, categorizing your expenses, allocating your income, and reviewing and adjusting your*

budget regularly, you can take control of your finances and work towards achieving your financial goals."

Building an Emergency Fund

In addition to creating a budget and setting financial goals, building an emergency fund is an important step towards mastering your personal finances. An emergency fund is a savings account that you can use to cover unexpected expenses, such as medical bills, car repairs, or job loss. Without an emergency fund, you may be forced to rely on credit cards or loans to cover these expenses, which can lead to debt and financial stress.

3.1. Setting a Savings Goal

The first step in building an emergency fund is to set a savings goal. Ideally, your emergency fund should cover three to six months of living expenses. To determine your living expenses, refer to your budget and add up your essential expenses, such as housing, utilities, food, and transportation. Multiply this amount by three to six to determine your savings goal.

3.2. Finding Room in Your Budget

Once you have set a savings goal, look for ways to find room in your budget to save towards your emergency fund. Consider reducing your non-essential expenses, such as entertainment and dining out, and redirecting that money towards your emergency fund. You may also need to adjust your financial goals to prioritize building your emergency fund.

3.3. Choosing the Right Savings Account

When building an emergency fund, it's important to choose the right savings account. Look for a high-yield savings account that offers a competitive interest rate and no fees. Consider setting up automatic transfers from your checking account to your savings account to make saving easier.

3.4. Staying Committed to Your Savings Goal

Building an emergency fund takes time and commitment. It's important to stay committed to your savings goal and make regular contributions to your emergency fund. Consider setting up a separate savings account specifically for your emergency fund to help you stay focused on your goal.

3.5. Using Your Emergency Fund

In the event of an emergency, it's important to use your emergency fund wisely. Only use your emergency fund for true emergencies, such as unexpected medical bills or job loss. Avoid using your emergency fund for non-essential expenses, such as vacations or shopping.

"Building an emergency fund is an important step towards mastering your personal finances. By setting a savings goal, finding room in your budget, choosing the right savings account, staying committed to your savings goal, and using your emergency fund wisely, you can prepare for unexpected expenses and achieve financial security."

Understanding Credit Scores and Reports

Credit scores and reports play a critical role in your financial life. Your credit score is a three-digit number that represents your creditworthiness, or the likelihood that you will repay debt on time. Your credit report is a detailed record of your credit history, including your credit accounts, payment history, and outstanding debts. Understanding your credit scores and reports is essential for managing your personal finances and achieving your financial goals.

4.1. Checking Your Credit Report

The first step in understanding your credit scores and reports is to check your credit report. You are entitled to a free credit report from each of the three major credit bureaus – Equifax, Experian, and TransUnion – once a year. Review your credit report carefully for errors, such as incorrect account information or late payments that you have already made.

4.2. Understanding Your Credit Score

Your credit score is calculated based on several factors, including your payment history, credit utilization, length of credit history, and types of credit accounts. The most used credit score is the FICO score, which ranges from 300 to 850. A higher score indicates a better creditworthiness and may result in lower interest rates and better credit offers.

4.3. Improving Your Credit Score

If your credit score is lower than you would like, there are several steps you can take to improve it. Start by making all your payments on time and reducing your credit utilization, or the amount of credit you are using compared to your credit limit. Avoid opening new credit accounts unless necessary and keep old accounts open to maintain a longer credit history.

4.4. Managing Your Credit Accounts

Managing your credit accounts is also important for maintaining a good credit score. Make sure to use your credit accounts responsibly, only borrowing what you can afford to repay on time. Avoid maxing out your credit cards and try to pay off your balances in full each month. If you do carry a balance, aim to keep it below 30% of your credit limit.

4.5. Monitoring Your Credit Report

Finally, it's important to monitor your credit report regularly for any changes or errors. Set up alerts with your credit card companies or credit monitoring services to notify you of any suspicious activity. By catching errors or fraudulent activity early, you can take steps to correct them and protect your credit score.

"UNDERSTANDING YOUR CREDIT SCORES AND REPORTS IS CRUCIAL FOR MANAGING YOUR PERSONAL FINANCES AND ACHIEVING YOUR FINANCIAL GOALS. BY CHECKING YOUR CREDIT REPORT, UNDERSTANDING YOUR CREDIT SCORE, IMPROVING YOUR CREDIT SCORE, MANAGING YOUR CREDIT ACCOUNTS, AND MONITORING YOUR CREDIT REPORT, YOU CAN TAKE CONTROL OF YOUR CREDIT AND ACHIEVE FINANCIAL SECURITY."

Chapter 2: Managing Debt

In this chapter, we will explore different types of debt, strategies for paying off debt, consolidation options, and dealing with collection agencies.

Different Types of Debt

Debt is an integral part of personal finance, and it can either be good or bad. Good debt helps you achieve financial goals such as investing in a home, getting an education, or starting a business. On the other hand, bad debt can cripple your finances, make it difficult to achieve your financial goals, and damage your credit score.

In this chapter, we will discuss the different types of debt and how you can manage them effectively.

1.1. Credit Card Debt

Credit card debt is one of the most common types of debt. It is unsecured debt, which means that there is no collateral attached to it. Credit cards usually have high-interest rates, and if not managed well, can quickly accumulate, and become overwhelming. To manage your credit card debt, you need to create a budget, pay more than the minimum payment required, and avoid using credit cards for impulse purchases.

1.2. Student Loans

Student loans are a type of debt that you acquire when you borrow money to pay for education. They can either be federal or private. Federal loans usually have lower interest rates and more flexible repayment options than private loans. To manage your student loans effectively, you need to understand the terms of your loans, make your payments on time, and explore options such as income-driven repayment plans or loan forgiveness programs.

1.3. Mortgage Loans

A mortgage is a type of debt that you incur when you borrow money to buy a home. Mortgages usually have lower interest rates than other types of debt, and the interest you pay may be tax-deductible. To manage your mortgage effectively, you need to make your payments on time, consider refinancing if you can get a lower interest rate, and avoid borrowing against the equity in your home.

1.4. Personal Loans

Personal loans are unsecured loans that you can use for a variety of purposes, such as consolidating debt, paying for a vacation, or financing a wedding. They usually have higher interest rates than other types of debt, and the interest is not tax-deductible. To manage your personal loans, you need to understand the terms of your loans, make your payments on time, and avoid using them for unnecessary expenses.

1.5. Auto Loans

Auto loans are a type of secured debt that you acquire when you borrow money to buy a car. The car itself serves as collateral, which means that if you fail to make your payments, the lender can repossess the car. To manage your auto loans, you need to understand the terms of your loans, make your payments on time, and avoid taking out a loan for a car that you cannot afford.

"IN SUMMARY, MANAGING DEBT IS AN ESSENTIAL ASPECT OF PERSONAL FINANCE. TO MANAGE YOUR DEBT EFFECTIVELY, YOU NEED TO UNDERSTAND THE DIFFERENT TYPES OF DEBT AND HOW THEY WORK, CREATE A BUDGET, MAKE YOUR PAYMENTS ON TIME, AND AVOID TAKING ON UNNECESSARY DEBT."

BY FOLLOWING THESE TIPS, YOU CAN TAKE CONTROL OF YOUR FINANCES AND ACHIEVE YOUR FINANCIAL GOALS.

Strategies for Paying Off Debt

Now that you understand the different types of debt, it's important to have a plan for paying them off. Here are some strategies you can use to pay off your debt:

2.1. Snowball Method

The snowball method involves paying off your debts in order from smallest to largest. Start by making the minimum payments on all your debts except the smallest one, which you'll put as much extra money as you can towards. Once you pay off the smallest debt, take the amount you were paying towards it and add it to the payment for the next smallest debt. Keep repeating this process until all your debts are paid off.

2.2. Avalanche Method

The avalanche method involves paying off your debts in order from highest interest rate to lowest interest rate. Start by making the minimum payments on all your debts except the one with the highest interest rate, which you'll put as much extra money as you can towards. Once you pay off the debt with the highest interest rate, take the amount you were paying towards it and add it to the payment for the debt with the next highest interest rate.

Keep repeating this process until all your debts are paid off.

2.3. Debt Consolidation

Debt consolidation involves combining all your debts into one loan or credit card with a lower interest rate. This can make it easier to manage your debt because you only have one payment to make each month. However, it's important to make sure the interest rate on the new loan or credit card is lower than the interest rates on your existing debts.

2.4. Negotiating with Creditors

You can also try negotiating with your creditors to see if they're willing to lower your interest rates or create a payment plan that's more manageable for you. This can be especially helpful if you're struggling to make your minimum payments.

2.5. Increasing Income

If you're having trouble making your minimum payments, consider finding ways to increase your income. This could include taking on a part-time job, selling items you no longer need, or starting a side business.

"REMEMBER, PAYING OFF DEBT TAKES TIME AND EFFORT. THE KEY IS TO CREATE A PLAN THAT WORKS FOR YOU AND STICK TO IT."

BY USING ONE OR MORE OF THESE STRATEGIES, YOU CAN PAY OFF YOUR DEBT AND ACHIEVE FINANCIAL FREEDOM.

Consolidation Options

If you're struggling to manage multiple debts with high interest rates, debt consolidation may be a good option for you. Here are some consolidation options to consider:

3.1. Balance Transfer Credit Cards

Balance transfer credit cards allow you to transfer your existing credit card balances to a new card with a lower interest rate. Many balance transfer cards offer 0% interest for a certain period, which can help you save money on interest payments. However, it's important to make sure you can pay off the balance before the promotional period ends, as the interest rate may increase significantly after that.

3.2. Personal Loans

Personal loans are unsecured loans that you can use to pay off your existing debt. The interest rate on personal loans is usually lower than credit card interest rates, which can save you money over time. However, personal loans may come with origination fees or prepayment penalties, so it's important to read the terms carefully before signing up.

3.3. Home Equity Loans

Home equity loans allow you to borrow against the equity in your home. The interest rate on home equity loans is usually lower than credit card interest rates, and the interest may be tax-deductible. However, if you fail to make your payments, you risk losing your home.

3.4. Retirement Account Loans

Some retirement accounts allow you to borrow against your balance. While this may be an option for some people, it's generally not recommended, as it can jeopardize your retirement savings and come with high fees.

3.5. Debt Management Plans

Debt management plans are offered by credit counselling agencies. They involve negotiating with your creditors to lower your interest rates and create a payment plan that's more manageable for you. You'll make one monthly payment to the credit counseling agency, which will then distribute the funds to your creditors.

"DEBT CONSOLIDATION CAN BE A HELPFUL TOOL FOR MANAGING MULTIPLE DEBTS WITH HIGH INTEREST RATES. HOWEVER, IT'S IMPORTANT TO WEIGH THE PROS AND CONS OF EACH OPTION AND READ THE TERMS CAREFULLY BEFORE SIGNING UP."

WITH A CONSOLIDATION PLAN IN PLACE, YOU CAN REDUCE YOUR INTEREST PAYMENTS AND PAY OFF YOUR DEBT MORE QUICKLY.

Dealing with Collection Agencies

If you've fallen behind on your debt payments, you may receive calls or letters from collection agencies. Here are some tips for dealing with collection agencies:

4.1. Know Your Rights

Under the Fair Debt Collection Practices Act (FDCPA), collection agencies are prohibited from using abusive or deceptive tactics to collect a debt. They must also provide you with certain information, such as the amount of the debt and the name of the original creditor. Be sure to familiarize yourself with your rights under the FDCPA so you can protect yourself from harassment or unfair practices.

4.2. Communicate in Writing

It's a good idea to communicate with collection agencies in writing, rather than over the phone. This allows you to keep a record of all correspondence and ensures that you have a clear paper trail if any issues arise. When you communicate in writing, be sure to keep your tone professional and avoid making any threats or admissions of guilt.

4.3. Negotiate a Payment Plan

If you're unable to pay off your debt in full, you may be able to negotiate a payment plan with the collection agency. Be sure to get any agreement in writing and read the terms carefully before agreeing to anything. Keep in mind that the collection agency may be willing to settle for less than the full amount if you can make a lump-sum payment.

4.4. Dispute the Debt

If you believe that the debt is not yours, or that the collection agency is attempting to collect an amount that is incorrect, you can dispute the debt in writing. The collection agency is required to investigate your dispute and provide you with a response.

4.5. Seek Legal Advice

If you're unsure about how to handle a collection agency or if you feel that your rights are being violated, it may be a good idea to seek legal advice. An attorney who specializes in debt collection can help you understand your options and protect your rights.

"DEALING WITH COLLECTION AGENCIES CAN BE STRESSFUL AND INTIMIDATING, BUT IT'S IMPORTANT TO REMEMBER THAT YOU HAVE RIGHTS UNDER THE LAW."

BY COMMUNICATING IN WRITING, NEGOTIATING A PAYMENT PLAN, AND SEEKING LEGAL ADVICE IF NECESSARY, YOU CAN PROTECT YOURSELF FROM UNFAIR OR ABUSIVE PRACTICES AND WORK TOWARDS RESOLVING YOUR DEBT.

Chapter 3: Saving and Investing

In this chapter, we will discuss the importance of saving, types of savings accounts, investing basics, and investing for retirement.

Importance of Saving

Saving is an essential component of personal finance management. It is the process of setting aside money for future use or emergencies. Saving can help you achieve your financial goals, whether it is buying a house, starting a business, or retiring comfortably. In this chapter, we will explore the importance of saving and how to save effectively.

1.1. Emergency Fund

One of the most important reasons to save is to build an emergency fund. An emergency fund is a pool of money set aside to cover unexpected expenses such as medical bills, car repairs, or job loss. Having an emergency fund can give you peace of mind and protect you from going into debt. Experts recommend having at least three to six months' worth of living expenses saved in an emergency fund.

1.2. Achieving Financial Goals

Saving can also help you achieve your financial goals. Whether it is saving for a down payment on a house or starting a business, saving regularly can help you reach your goals faster. Setting specific goals and creating a savings plan can help you stay on track and motivated.

1.3. Retirement

Saving for retirement is another critical reason to save. Retirement can be expensive, and Social Security benefits may not be enough to cover all your expenses. Starting early and saving consistently can help you build a nest egg for retirement. Compound interest can also work in your favour, allowing your savings to grow over time.

1.4. Rainy Day Fund

Apart from emergency funds, having a rainy-day fund is also important. It is a separate savings account used for irregular expenses such as vacations, home repairs, or unexpected opportunities. Having a rainy-day fund can help you avoid dipping into your emergency fund or going into debt.

1.5.   Avoiding Debt

Saving can also help you avoid debt. When you have money set aside for unexpected expenses, you are less likely to rely on credit cards or loans. This can help you save money on interest and fees, and keep you from falling into a debt trap.

"SAVING IS A CRUCIAL ASPECT OF PERSONAL FINANCE. IT CAN HELP YOU BUILD AN EMERGENCY FUND, ACHIEVE YOUR FINANCIAL GOALS, SAVE FOR RETIREMENT, AVOID DEBT, AND PROVIDE A SENSE OF FINANCIAL SECURITY."

IN THE NEXT SECTION, WE WILL DISCUSS THE DIFFERENT TYPES OF SAVINGS ACCOUNTS AND HOW TO CHOOSE THE RIGHT ONE FOR YOU.

Types of Savings Accounts

There are several types of savings accounts available, each with its own features and benefits. Here are some of the most common types of savings accounts:

2.1. Traditional savings accounts

These accounts are offered by banks and credit unions and typically pay a low interest rate. They are a good option for short-term savings or emergency funds. Traditional savings accounts are FDIC-insured, which means that your money is protected up to $250,000.

2.2. High-yield savings accounts

High-yield savings accounts are similar to traditional savings accounts, but they offer higher interest rates. These accounts typically require a minimum balance and may have restrictions on withdrawals. High-yield savings accounts are also FDIC-insured.

2.3. Money market accounts

Money market accounts are similar to savings accounts but typically offer higher interest rates. They also allow you to write checks and use a debit card, making them more flexible than traditional savings accounts. Money market accounts are FDIC-insured.

2.4. Certificates of deposit (CDs)

CDs are a type of savings account that requires you to deposit your money for a set period, usually ranging from a few months to several years. CDs typically offer higher interest rates than traditional savings accounts, but you cannot withdraw your money before the term is up without penalty. CDs are also FDIC-insured.

2.5. Individual retirement accounts (IRAs)

IRAs are savings accounts designed specifically for retirement savings. They offer tax advantages and can be opened at a bank, credit union, or brokerage firm. There are two main types of IRAs: traditional and Roth. With a traditional IRA, you make pre-tax contributions, and your money grows tax-deferred until you withdraw it in retirement. With a Roth IRA, you make after-tax contributions, and your money grows tax-free.

"CHOOSING THE RIGHT TYPE OF SAVINGS ACCOUNT DEPENDS ON YOUR FINANCIAL GOALS AND HOW MUCH ACCESS YOU NEED TO YOUR MONEY. WHEN COMPARING SAVINGS ACCOUNTS, BE SURE TO CONSIDER THE INTEREST RATE, FEES, MINIMUM BALANCE REQUIREMENTS, AND ANY RESTRICTIONS ON WITHDRAWALS."

BY CHOOSING THE RIGHT SAVINGS ACCOUNT, YOU CAN MAKE YOUR MONEY WORK HARDER FOR YOU AND ACHIEVE YOUR FINANCIAL GOALS FASTER.

Investing Basics

Investing is a crucial part of personal finance that can help you build wealth and achieve your long-term financial goals. Here are some investing basics to keep in mind:

3.1. Start Early

One of the most important things you can do is to start investing early. The earlier you start, the more time your investments have to grow. Even small amounts can make a big difference over time, thanks to the power of compound interest.

3.2. Diversify

Diversification is key to a successful investment strategy. It means spreading your money across different types of investments, such as stocks, bonds, and mutual funds. This can help reduce your overall risk and protect your portfolio from market fluctuations.

3.3. Set Goals

Before you start investing, it's important to set clear goals. Do you want to save for a down payment on a house, pay for your children's education, or retire comfortably? Knowing your goals can help you create a personalized investment plan.

3.4. Manage Risk

All investments come with some level of risk, but it's important to manage that risk. This means understanding the risks associated with each investment and making informed decisions. Avoid putting all your money in one investment or chasing hot stocks, which can be risky.

3.5. Monitor your Investments

Once you have started investing, it's important to monitor your investments regularly. This means keeping an eye on market trends, reviewing your portfolio periodically, and rebalancing your investments as needed.

3.6. Seek professional Advice

Investing can be complex, and it's important to seek professional advice if you are unsure about where to start or how to manage your investments. A financial advisor can help you create a personalized investment plan that takes your goals, risk tolerance, and time horizon into account.

"INVESTING IS AN IMPORTANT PART OF PERSONAL FINANCE THAT CAN HELP YOU BUILD WEALTH AND ACHIEVE YOUR FINANCIAL GOALS."

BY FOLLOWING THESE INVESTING BASICS, YOU CAN CREATE A SUCCESSFUL INVESTMENT STRATEGY THAT WORKS FOR YOU. HOWEVER, KEEP IN MIND THAT INVESTING ALWAYS CARRIES RISK, SO IT'S IMPORTANT TO BE INFORMED AND MAKE INFORMED DECISIONS.

Investing for Retirement

Investing for retirement is one of the most important long-term financial goals you can have. Here are some tips for investing for retirement:

4.1. Start Early

As mentioned earlier, starting early is key to successful investing. The earlier you start investing for retirement, the more time your investments have to grow. This can help you save more for retirement and potentially retire earlier.

4.2. Consider tax-advantaged retirement Accounts

Tax-advantaged retirement accounts, such as traditional and Roth IRAs, 401(k)s, and 403(b)s, offer tax benefits that can help you save more for retirement. Contributions to these accounts may be tax-deductible or grow tax-free, depending on the account type. Consider maxing out your contributions to take advantage of these benefits.

4.3. Choose the right Investments

Choosing the right investments is crucial when investing for retirement. You may want to consider low-cost index funds or mutual funds, which can provide diversification and potentially higher returns over time. However, keep in mind that all investments come with some level of risk, so it's important to manage that risk.

4.4. Rebalance your portfolio Periodically

As you get closer to retirement, it's important to rebalance your portfolio periodically to ensure that it aligns with your retirement goals and risk tolerance. This means adjusting the mix of investments to ensure that you have the right balance of stocks, bonds, and other assets.

4.5. Plan for withdrawals in retirement

Finally, it's important to plan for withdrawals in retirement. This means determining how much you will need to withdraw each year to cover your living expenses and how your investments will generate that income. Consider working with a financial advisor to create a withdrawal plan that meets your needs.

"INVESTING FOR RETIREMENT IS A LONG-TERM FINANCIAL GOAL THAT REQUIRES CAREFUL PLANNING AND MANAGEMENT."

BY STARTING EARLY, CONSIDERING TAX-ADVANTAGED RETIREMENT ACCOUNTS, CHOOSING THE RIGHT INVESTMENTS, REBALANCING YOUR PORTFOLIO PERIODICALLY, AND PLANNING FOR WITHDRAWALS IN RETIREMENT, YOU CAN CREATE A SUCCESSFUL RETIREMENT INVESTMENT STRATEGY THAT HELPS YOU ACHIEVE YOUR GOALS.

Chapter 4: Making Money Work for You

In this chapter, we will cover strategies for increasing income, creating additional income streams, maximizing employee benefits, and starting a side business.

Strategies for Increasing Income

Having a solid financial foundation is essential, but sometimes the key to achieving financial stability is increasing your income. There are several strategies you can use to increase your income, some of which are outlined below:

1.1. Negotiate a Raise

If you have been at your job for a while and have a proven track record of success, consider negotiating a raise. You can make a case for your value to the company by highlighting your accomplishments, demonstrating your willingness to take on additional responsibilities, and showcasing your expertise.

1.2. Look for a Higher-Paying Job

If your current job isn't paying you what you're worth, it may be time to explore other job opportunities. Keep an eye out for job openings in your field that offer higher salaries or better benefits.

1.3. Freelance or Consult

If you have a particular skill set, consider freelancing or consulting in your spare time. This can be a great way to earn extra income while also developing your skills and building your network.

1.4. Sell Unused Items

Take a look around your home or apartment and identify any unused items that you could sell. This could include furniture, clothing, electronics, or other household items. You can sell these items online through sites like eBay or Craigslist, or hold a garage sale.

1.5. Participate in the Gig Economy

The gig economy has exploded in recent years, and there are a variety of platforms that allow you to earn money on your own terms. For example, you could become an Uber or Lyft driver, offer your services as a TaskRabbit, or rent out a spare room on Airbnb.

1.6. Develop a Passive Income Stream

A passive income stream is one that requires minimal effort to maintain, but continues to generate income over time. This could include investments, rental property, or online businesses that you can set up and run in your spare time.

1.7. Learn a New Skill

Finally, consider learning a new skill that will increase your value in the job market. This could include taking a course in coding or web design, learning a new language, or earning a certification in a particular field.

"BY USING ONE OR MORE OF THESE STRATEGIES, YOU CAN INCREASE YOUR INCOME AND IMPROVE YOUR FINANCIAL STABILITY."

REMEMBER, THE KEY IS TO BE PROACTIVE AND TAKE CONTROL OF YOUR FINANCIAL FUTURE.

Creating Additional Income Streams

In addition to increasing your income through your job or side hustles, creating additional income streams can provide a reliable source of passive income that can help you achieve financial freedom. Here are some strategies to consider:

2.1. Rent Out Your Property

If you own a property, renting it out can be a great way to generate passive income. This could include renting out a spare room on Airbnb, or renting out your entire property as a vacation rental.

2.2. Invest in Real Estate

Real estate investing can be a lucrative way to create additional income streams. You can invest in rental properties, or use platforms like Fundrise or Roofstock to invest in real estate without the hassle of property management.

2.3. Start a Blog or YouTube Channel

If you have a particular expertise or passion, consider starting a blog or YouTube channel. You can monetize your content through ads, sponsorships, or affiliate marketing.

2.4. Create an Online Course

Online learning is becoming increasingly popular, and creating an online course can be a great way to monetize your expertise. You can use platforms like Teachable or Udemy to create and sell your course.

2.5. Invest in Stocks, Bonds, or Mutual Funds

Investing in the stock market can be a great way to create passive income streams. You can invest in stocks, bonds, or mutual funds, and earn dividends or capital gains.

2.6. Create and Sell a Product

If you have a talent for creating products, consider selling them online through platforms like Etsy or Amazon. This could include handmade crafts, digital products, or physical products that you manufacture.

2.7.   Affiliate Marketing

Affiliate marketing is a way to earn commissions by promoting other people's products or services. You can promote products on your blog, social media, or through email marketing.

"CREATING ADDITIONAL INCOME STREAMS CAN PROVIDE FINANCIAL SECURITY AND FLEXIBILITY, AND CAN HELP YOU ACHIEVE YOUR FINANCIAL GOALS FASTER."

REMEMBER, THE KEY TO SUCCESS IS FINDING A STRATEGY THAT ALIGNS WITH YOUR SKILLS, INTERESTS, AND VALUES.

Maximizing Employee Benefits

In addition to increasing your income and creating additional income streams, maximizing your employee benefits can be a great way to improve your financial situation. Here are some strategies to consider:

3.1. Take Advantage of 401(k) Matching

If your employer offers a 401(k)-matching program, make sure you contribute enough to maximize the matching contribution. This is essentially free money, and can add up to thousands of dollars over time.

3.2. Sign Up for a Flexible Spending Account (FSA)

If your employer offers an FSA, take advantage of it. This allows you to contribute pre-tax dollars to pay for qualified medical expenses or dependent care expenses, saving you money on taxes.

3.3. Use Your Health Benefits

Many employers offer health benefits that go beyond just medical coverage. Take advantage of any wellness programs, gym memberships, or other health-related benefits that your employer offers.

3.4. Consider Disability Insurance

Disability insurance can provide financial protection if you become disabled and are unable to work. If your employer offers disability insurance, consider enrolling.

3.5. Use Your Vacation Time

It's important to take time off from work to recharge and avoid burnout. Make sure you use all of your vacation time each year, and consider taking advantage of any paid sick leave or personal days that your employer offers.

3.6. Take Advantage of Educational Benefits

Many employers offer educational benefits, such as tuition reimbursement or access to online courses. Take advantage of these opportunities to improve your skills and advance your career.

3.7. Review Your Benefits Annually

Finally, it's important to review your employee benefits annually to make sure you're taking advantage of everything that's available to you. Make sure you understand the benefits that your employer offers and ask questions if you're unsure about anything.

"MAXIMIZING YOUR EMPLOYEE BENEFITS CAN PROVIDE SIGNIFICANT FINANCIAL BENEFITS AND HELP YOU ACHIEVE YOUR LONG-TERM FINANCIAL GOALS."

BY TAKING ADVANTAGE OF THE BENEFITS THAT YOUR EMPLOYER OFFERS, YOU CAN SAVE MONEY ON TAXES, IMPROVE YOUR HEALTH AND WELL-BEING, AND BUILD A MORE SECURE FINANCIAL FUTURE.

Starting a Side Business

Starting a side business can be a great way to increase your income and achieve financial freedom. Here are some strategies to consider:

4.1.   Identify Your Skills and Interests

The first step in starting a side business is to identify your skills and interests. What are you good at? What do you enjoy doing? This will help you determine what type of business to start.

4.2.   Research Your Market

Once you've identified your skills and interests, research your market to determine if there's a demand for the product or service you're considering. Look at your competition, and determine what makes your product or service unique.

4.3.   Develop a Business Plan

A business plan will help you define your business goals, target market, pricing, and marketing strategies. This will help you stay focused and on track as you launch and grow your business.

4.4.   Start Small

Starting a side business doesn't have to be a huge investment. Start small, and focus on building your customer base and refining your product or service. As your business grows, you can invest more time and money into it.

4.5.   Use Online Platforms

There are many online platforms that can help you start and grow your business, such as Etsy, Amazon, and Shopify. These platforms provide an easy way to set up an online store and reach a large audience.

4.6. Leverage Your Network

Your network can be a valuable resource in starting and growing your business. Reach out to friends, family, and colleagues, and let them know about your business. Ask for referrals and feedback, and use their support to help you grow your business.

4.7. Stay Focused

Starting a side business requires hard work and dedication. Stay focused on your goals, and don't get discouraged by setbacks or challenges. Keep pushing forward and continue to refine your business as you learn and grow.

"STARTING A SIDE BUSINESS CAN BE A GREAT WAY TO ACHIEVE FINANCIAL FREEDOM AND PURSUE YOUR PASSIONS."

BY IDENTIFYING YOUR SKILLS AND INTERESTS, RESEARCHING YOUR MARKET, AND DEVELOPING A SOLID BUSINESS PLAN, YOU CAN START AND GROW A SUCCESSFUL

BUSINESS THAT PROVIDES A RELIABLE SOURCE OF INCOME.

Chapter 5: Protecting Your Wealth

In this chapter, we will discuss insurance basics, choosing the right insurance policies, estate planning, and tax planning.

Insurance Basics

Insurance is a tool that helps individuals protect themselves and their assets from unforeseen events. It can be overwhelming to navigate the different types of insurance policies, but understanding the basics can help you make informed decisions.

1.1 What is insurance?

Insurance is a contract between you and an insurance company. You pay a premium in exchange for protection against potential financial losses. The insurance company assumes the risk and provides financial support if the insured event occurs.

1.2 Types of Insurance

There are various types of insurance policies available, but some of the most common ones include:

- Health insurance: covers medical expenses in case of illness or injury.

- Life insurance: provides a lump sum payment to beneficiaries in case of the policyholder's death.

- Homeowner's insurance: protects against damage to your home or personal belongings due to events such as fire, theft, or natural disasters.

- Auto insurance: covers damages to your vehicle and liability for injuries or damages to other parties in case of an accident.

- Disability insurance: provides income replacement if you become disabled and cannot work.

- Long-term care insurance: covers the cost of long-term care services in case of a chronic illness or disability.

1.3 How Insurance Works

Insurance companies collect premiums from policyholders and use those funds to pay out claims for covered events. Insurance policies often have deductibles, which are the amount you must pay out of pocket before the insurance coverage kicks in.

The insurance company calculates premiums based on factors such as the type of coverage, the policyholder's age, health, occupation, and location. The higher the risk of a potential claim, the higher the premium.

1.4 How to Choose Insurance Policies

When choosing insurance policies, consider your specific needs and circumstances. It's essential to balance the cost of the policy with the amount of coverage it provides.

Before buying an insurance policy, read the fine print and make sure you understand what it covers and what it doesn't. Compare policies and prices from different providers and ask questions to clarify any doubts.

Choosing the Right Insurance Policies

Choosing the right insurance policies is crucial to ensure you have adequate coverage and protection for potential risks. Here are some factors to consider when selecting insurance policies:

2.1 Assess Your Risks

Before choosing insurance policies, assess your risks and determine the types of coverage you need. For example, if you have dependents, life insurance may be essential to provide financial support in case of your death. If you own a home, homeowner's insurance can protect your property and belongings.

Consider the potential costs of not having insurance coverage and balance that against the cost of the policy. For example, the cost of healthcare can be exorbitant without health insurance, so it's essential to have adequate coverage.

2.2 Understand the Policy Terms and Conditions

It's essential to read and understand the policy terms and conditions before purchasing insurance. This includes the coverage limits, deductibles, exclusions, and any conditions or requirements.

Make sure you know what the policy covers and what it doesn't. For example, a homeowner's insurance policy may cover damages from a storm but exclude damages from floods.

2.3 Research Insurance Companies

Research insurance companies to ensure they are reputable and financially stable. Check their ratings and reviews from third-party sources, such as J.D. Power and Associates, the Better Business Bureau, and online reviews.

Consider the company's history of paying claims promptly and fairly. Check if they have a good track record of resolving disputes with policyholders.

2.4 Compare Premiums and Deductibles

Compare premiums and deductibles from different insurance companies to find the best coverage for your budget. Keep in mind that a lower premium may come with a higher deductible, which means you'll pay more out of pocket before the insurance coverage kicks in.

Consider bundling insurance policies, such as combining home and auto insurance, to save on premiums. Ask about discounts for factors such as a good driving record or home security systems.

2.5 Seek Professional Advice

If you're unsure about which insurance policies to choose, seek advice from a professional, such as an insurance agent or financial advisor. They can help you understand your risks, assess your coverage needs, and recommend policies that suit your budget and goals.

"CHOOSING THE RIGHT INSURANCE POLICIES IS ESSENTIAL TO PROTECT YOURSELF AND YOUR ASSETS FROM POTENTIAL RISKS."

ASSESS YOUR RISKS, UNDERSTAND THE POLICY TERMS AND CONDITIONS, RESEARCH INSURANCE COMPANIES, COMPARE PREMIUMS AND DEDUCTIBLES, AND SEEK PROFESSIONAL ADVICE TO MAKE INFORMED DECISIONS AND SAFEGUARD YOUR WEALTH.

Estate Planning

Estate planning is an important aspect of protecting your wealth and ensuring your assets are distributed according to your wishes after your death. Here are some key considerations for estate planning:

3.1 Understand Estate Planning

Estate planning involves creating a plan for the distribution of your assets after your death. It involves legal documents, such as a will, trust, and power of attorney, to ensure your wishes are carried out.

Estate planning also includes considering factors such as taxes, beneficiaries, and potential guardians for minors. It's important to consult with a legal or financial professional to ensure your estate plan is legally valid and effective.

3.2 Create a Will

A will is a legal document that outlines how your assets will be distributed after your death. It's essential to create a will to ensure your wishes are followed and to avoid disputes among family members.

Your will should name an executor, who is responsible for carrying out your wishes and settling your affairs. It should also name beneficiaries and specify how your assets will be divided.

It's important to update your will regularly, especially after major life events such as marriage, divorce, or the birth of a child.

3.3 Consider a Trust

A trust is a legal document that allows you to transfer assets to a trustee, who manages them for the benefit of beneficiaries. Trusts can provide tax benefits and allow for more control over how assets are distributed.

There are different types of trusts, such as revocable and irrevocable trusts. Consult with a legal or financial professional to determine which type of trust is best for your situation.

3.4 Choose Beneficiaries Carefully

Choosing beneficiaries is an important part of estate planning. Consider factors such as age, financial responsibility, and relationship when selecting beneficiaries.

It's also essential to keep beneficiary designations up to date, especially for assets such as life insurance policies and retirement accounts.

3.5 Plan for Incapacity

In addition to planning for after your death, it's important to plan for incapacity. This includes creating a power of attorney, which designates someone to make financial and legal decisions on your behalf if you become unable to do so.

It's also essential to have advance directives, such as a living will or healthcare proxy, which outlines your wishes for medical care and end-of-life decisions.

"ESTATE PLANNING IS AN IMPORTANT ASPECT OF PROTECTING YOUR WEALTH AND ENSURING

YOUR ASSETS ARE DISTRIBUTED ACCORDING TO YOUR WISHES."

CREATE A WILL, CONSIDER A TRUST, CHOOSE BENEFICIARIES CAREFULLY, PLAN FOR INCAPACITY, AND CONSULT WITH A LEGAL OR FINANCIAL PROFESSIONAL TO ENSURE YOUR ESTATE PLAN IS LEGALLY VALID AND EFFECTIVE.

Tax Planning

Tax planning is an important aspect of managing your personal finances and protecting your wealth. Here are some key considerations for tax planning:

4.1 Understand Tax Laws

Understanding tax laws is essential for effective tax planning. Stay informed about changes in tax laws and regulations and consult with a tax professional to ensure you're maximizing your tax benefits and minimizing your tax liabilities.

Take advantage of tax deductions and credits, such as those for charitable donations, education expenses, and home mortgage interest. Keep thorough records and receipts to support your deductions and avoid audits.

4.2 Maximize Retirement Savings

Contributing to retirement accounts, such as a 401(k) or IRA, is a smart way to save for retirement and reduce your tax liability. These accounts offer tax-deferred growth and may also provide tax deductions or credits for contributions.

Consider maximizing your contributions to these accounts, especially if your employer offers matching contributions. Consult with a financial advisor to determine the best retirement savings strategy for your goals and needs.

4.3 Consider Tax-Efficient Investments

Investing in tax-efficient investments, such as index funds or municipal bonds, can help reduce your tax liability.

These investments are designed to minimize taxable events, such as capital gains, and provide tax-free income.

Consult with a financial advisor to determine which tax-efficient investments are best for your goals and risk tolerance.

4.4 Plan for Estate Taxes

Estate taxes can significantly reduce the value of your estate and impact your beneficiaries' inheritance. Estate planning, such as creating a trust or gifting assets, can help minimize estate taxes.

Consult with a legal or financial professional to determine the best estate planning strategy for your situation and goals.

4.5 Stay Organized

Staying organized is crucial for effective tax planning. Keep thorough records of your income, expenses, and deductions and stay up to date on deadlines for tax filings and payments.

Consider using tax preparation software or consulting with a tax professional to ensure accuracy and maximize your tax benefits.

"TAX PLANNING IS AN IMPORTANT ASPECT OF MANAGING YOUR PERSONAL FINANCES AND PROTECTING YOUR WEALTH. UNDERSTAND TAX LAWS, MAXIMIZE RETIREMENT SAVINGS, CONSIDER TAX-EFFICIENT INVESTMENTS, PLAN FOR ESTATE TAXES, AND STAY ORGANIZED TO ENSURE YOU'RE MAXIMIZING YOUR TAX BENEFITS AND MINIMIZING YOUR TAX LIABILITIES."

CONSULT WITH A TAX PROFESSIONAL OR FINANCIAL ADVISOR FOR PERSONALIZED GUIDANCE AND SUPPORT.

Chapter 6: Planning for the Future

In this chapter, we will explore retirement planning,

setting financial goals, creating a long-term financial

plan, and monitoring and adjusting your plan.

Retirement Planning

Retirement is a time when we want to relax and enjoy the fruits of our labour. However, this is only possible if we plan ahead and prepare ourselves financially for this stage in life. Retirement planning is essential for everyone, regardless of their age or income. In this chapter, we will discuss the key elements of retirement planning and how to create a retirement plan that suits your goals.

1.1. Setting Retirement Goals

The first step in retirement planning is to set your retirement goals. These goals should be realistic and specific, such as the age you want to retire, the lifestyle you want to maintain, and the activities you want to enjoy during retirement. Once you have set your retirement goals, you can work towards achieving them.

1.2. Calculating Retirement Income

One of the most important aspects of retirement planning is calculating your retirement income. This involves estimating your retirement expenses and determining how much income you will need to cover them. You can use online calculators, financial advisors, or retirement planning software to help you with this process. It's essential to factor in inflation and any unexpected expenses that may arise.

1.3. Maximizing Retirement Savings

Another key component of retirement planning is maximizing your retirement savings. There are several retirement accounts available, such as 401(k), IRA, and Roth IRA. These accounts offer tax benefits and allow your money to grow tax-free or tax-deferred, depending on the account type. It's crucial to start saving for retirement as early as possible, even if it's a small amount. Over time, these small contributions can add up significantly.

1.4. Creating a Retirement Plan

Once you have calculated your retirement income and maximized your retirement savings, it's time to create a retirement plan. This plan should outline how you will achieve your retirement goals and the steps you need to take to get there. It should also consider the risks associated with retirement, such as market volatility, inflation, and longevity risk.

1.5. Managing Retirement Risks

Managing retirement risks is an essential part of retirement planning. These risks can impact your retirement income and your ability to achieve your retirement goals. It's important to have a diversified retirement portfolio that balances risk and return. It's also essential to have insurance coverage, such as health insurance, long-term care insurance, and life insurance, to protect your retirement income and assets.

1.6. Adjusting Your Retirement Plan

Finally, it's important to regularly review and adjust your retirement plan as needed. Your retirement goals may change over time, and external factors, such as economic conditions, can impact your retirement plan. It's important to be flexible and make changes when necessary to ensure that your retirement plan continues to meet your goals and needs.

"RETIREMENT PLANNING IS CRUCIAL TO ACHIEVING A COMFORTABLE AND ENJOYABLE RETIREMENT. BY SETTING REALISTIC GOALS, CALCULATING YOUR RETIREMENT INCOME, MAXIMIZING YOUR RETIREMENT SAVINGS, CREATING A RETIREMENT PLAN, MANAGING RETIREMENT RISKS, AND ADJUSTING YOUR PLAN AS NEEDED, YOU CAN ENSURE THAT YOU ACHIEVE YOUR RETIREMENT GOALS AND ENJOY A FINANCIALLY SECURE RETIREMENT."

START PLANNING TODAY AND TAKE CONTROL OF YOUR FINANCIAL FUTURE.

Setting Financial Goals

When it comes to retirement planning, setting financial goals is a crucial step in the process. Here are some tips for setting effective financial goals for your retirement plan:

2.1. Be Specific

Set specific goals that are tailored to your retirement needs. Instead of setting a vague goal like "save more money," set a specific goal such as "save $500 a month for retirement."

2.2. Be Realistic

Set realistic goals that are achievable. Be honest with yourself about your financial situation, and set goals that you can realistically meet.

2.3. Prioritize Goals

Prioritize your goals based on their importance. For example, if retiring at a certain age is important to you, prioritize that goal over other goals such as buying a vacation home.

2.4. Break Down Goals

Break down your goals into smaller, manageable steps. This can help you stay motivated and track your progress towards your goals.

2.5. Consider Your Timeline

Consider your timeline for achieving your goals. If you have a longer time horizon before retirement, you may have more flexibility in your investment choices. If you have a shorter timeline, you may need to adjust your goals and investment strategy accordingly.

2.6. Review and Adjust Goals

Regularly review and adjust your goals as needed. Life circumstances and market conditions can change, so it's important to be flexible and make changes to your goals and retirement plan as needed.

"BY SETTING EFFECTIVE FINANCIAL GOALS FOR YOUR RETIREMENT PLAN, YOU CAN ENSURE THAT YOU STAY ON TRACK AND ACHIEVE THE

*RETIREMENT LIFESTYLE THAT YOU DESIRE.
REMEMBER TO BE SPECIFIC, REALISTIC,
PRIORITIZE YOUR GOALS, BREAK THEM DOWN
INTO MANAGEABLE STEPS, CONSIDER YOUR
TIMELINE, AND REGULARLY REVIEW AND
ADJUST YOUR GOALS."*

*WITH THESE TIPS IN MIND, YOU CAN CREATE A
RETIREMENT PLAN THAT WILL HELP YOU
ACHIEVE FINANCIAL SECURITY AND A
COMFORTABLE RETIREMENT.*

Creating a Long-Term Financial Plan

Retirement planning is just one aspect of a comprehensive long-term financial plan. A long-term financial plan should consider your current financial situation and your goals for the future. Here are some tips for creating a comprehensive long-term financial plan:

3.1.   Assess Your Current Financial Situation

Start by assessing your current financial situation. This includes evaluating your income, expenses, debt, savings, and investments. Use this information as a starting point for creating your long-term financial plan.

3.2. Set Short-Term and Long-Term Goals

Set both short-term and long-term financial goals that are specific, measurable, and achievable. Short-term goals may include paying off debt, while long-term goals may include saving for retirement or buying a home.

3.3. Create a Budget

Create a budget that takes into account your income, expenses, and financial goals. Your budget should be realistic and reflect your priorities.

3.4. Maximize Your Savings

Maximize your savings by taking advantage of tax-advantaged retirement accounts, such as a 401(k) or IRA, and automating your savings contributions.

3.5. Invest Wisely

Invest wisely by creating a diversified investment portfolio that matches your risk tolerance and financial goals. Consider working with a financial advisor to create an investment strategy that works for you.

3.6. Manage Your Debt

Manage your debt by creating a debt repayment plan and prioritizing high-interest debt. Avoid taking on new debt that may hinder your progress towards your long-term financial goals.

3.7. Protect Your Assets

Protect your assets by obtaining appropriate insurance coverage, such as health insurance, life insurance, and disability insurance.

3.8. Review and Adjust Your Plan

Regularly review and adjust your long-term financial plan as needed. Life circumstances and market conditions can change, so it's important to be flexible and make changes to your plan as needed.

"BY CREATING A COMPREHENSIVE LONG-TERM FINANCIAL PLAN, YOU CAN ACHIEVE FINANCIAL SECURITY AND REACH YOUR FINANCIAL GOALS. REMEMBER TO ASSESS YOUR CURRENT FINANCIAL SITUATION, SET SHORT-TERM AND LONG-TERM GOALS, CREATE A BUDGET, MAXIMIZE YOUR SAVINGS, INVEST WISELY, MANAGE YOUR DEBT, PROTECT YOUR ASSETS, AND REGULARLY REVIEW AND ADJUST YOUR PLAN."

WITH THESE TIPS IN MIND, YOU CAN CREATE A LONG-TERM FINANCIAL PLAN THAT WORKS FOR YOU AND HELPS YOU ACHIEVE YOUR FINANCIAL GOALS.

Monitoring and Adjusting Your Plan

Creating a long-term financial plan is an important step towards achieving your financial goals, but it's not a one-time event. To ensure that you stay on track, it's important to regularly monitor and adjust your plan as needed. Here are some tips for monitoring and adjusting your long-term financial plan:

4.1. Regularly Review Your Plan

Set a regular schedule to review your long-term financial plan. This may be quarterly, semi-annually, or annually, depending on your needs. During the review, assess your progress towards your financial goals and make any necessary adjustments.

4.2. Monitor Your Investments

Monitor your investments regularly to ensure that they are performing as expected. Consider rebalancing your investment portfolio periodically to maintain a diversified allocation that matches your risk tolerance and financial goals.

4.3. Evaluate Your Budget

Evaluate your budget periodically to ensure that it reflects your current financial situation and goals. Adjust your budget as needed to stay on track towards your financial goals.

4.4. Reassess Your Risk Tolerance

Reassess your risk tolerance periodically to ensure that your investment strategy matches your risk tolerance and financial goals. As you approach retirement, you may need to adjust your investment strategy to reduce risk and protect your assets.

4.5. Adjust Your Goals

Life circumstances can change, and your financial goals may need to be adjusted accordingly. For example, a change in income, a new job, or a major life event may require you to adjust your financial goals and your long-term financial plan.

4.6.   Seek Professional Advice

Consider working with a financial advisor to help you monitor and adjust your long-term financial plan. A financial advisor can provide objective advice and help you make informed decisions about your investments, budget, and financial goals.

"By regularly monitoring and adjusting your long-term financial plan, you can ensure that you stay on track towards achieving your financial goals. Remember to regularly review your plan, monitor your investments, evaluate your budget, reassess your risk tolerance, adjust your goals, and seek professional advice as needed."

With these tips in mind, you can create a long-term financial plan that adapts to your changing needs and helps you achieve financial security and a comfortable retirement.

Chapter 7: Conclusion

In the final chapter, we will recap the key points covered in the book and encourage you to take action towards improving your financial situation. We will also provide resources for further learning and offer final thoughts on the importance of mastering your personal finances

Recap of Key Points

Congratulations, you have reached the end of "Money Moves: Mastering Your Personal Finances"! Throughout this book, we've covered a lot of ground, from building a strong financial foundation to protecting your wealth and planning for the future. Let's recap the key points of each chapter to reinforce what you've learned.

In Chapter 1, we discussed the importance of understanding your financial situation, creating a budget, building an emergency fund, and monitoring your credit score and reports. These are the building blocks for financial success and will help you stay on track with your goals.

In Chapter 2, we talked about managing debt, including strategies for paying off debt, consolidation options, and dealing with collection agencies. By taking control of your debt, you can free up money for other financial goals and reduce stress.

In Chapter 3, we explored saving and investing, including the importance of saving, different types of savings accounts, investing basics, and investing for retirement. By saving and investing wisely, you can build wealth and achieve financial security.

In Chapter 4, we discussed strategies for increasing income, creating additional income streams, maximizing employee benefits, and starting a side business. By making your money work for you, you can achieve your financial goals faster.

In Chapter 5, we covered protecting your wealth, including insurance basics, choosing the right insurance policies, estate planning, and tax planning. By protecting your wealth, you can safeguard against unexpected events and ensure that your assets are distributed according to your wishes.

In Chapter 6, we talked about planning for the future, including retirement planning, setting financial goals, creating a long-term financial plan, and monitoring and adjusting your plan. By planning for the future, you can ensure that you're on track to achieve your goals and make any necessary adjustments along the way.

IN CONCLUSION, "MONEY MOVES: MASTERING YOUR PERSONAL FINANCES" IS A COMPREHENSIVE GUIDE TO TAKING CONTROL OF YOUR FINANCES AND ACHIEVING FINANCIAL SUCCESS. BY FOLLOWING THE STEPS OUTLINED IN THIS BOOK, YOU CAN BUILD A STRONG FINANCIAL FOUNDATION, MANAGE DEBT, SAVE AND INVEST WISELY, MAKE YOUR MONEY WORK FOR YOU, PROTECT YOUR WEALTH, AND PLAN FOR THE FUTURE.

REMEMBER, FINANCIAL SUCCESS IS WITHIN YOUR REACH - IT JUST TAKES A LITTLE KNOWLEDGE, PLANNING, AND DISCIPLINE. BEST OF LUCK ON YOUR FINANCIAL JOURNEY!

Encouragement to Take Action

Now that you have read "Money Moves: Mastering Your Personal Finances," you have the knowledge and tools to take control of your financial future. But knowledge alone is not enough - it's what you do with that knowledge that matters.

The key to financial success is taking action, and there's no better time to start than now. It's easy to feel overwhelmed by the enormity of the task, but remember that every small step you take is a step in the right direction.

Here are some tips to help you take action and start making progress towards your financial goals:

1. Set achievable goals - Start by setting realistic, achievable goals that you can work towards. Break them down into smaller steps to make them more manageable.

2. Create a plan - Develop a plan that outlines the steps you need to take to achieve your goals. Make sure your plan is specific, measurable, and time-bound.

3. Take small steps - Start by taking small steps towards your goals. It's important to build momentum and gain confidence as you go.

4. Stay motivated - Celebrate your progress and stay motivated by tracking your successes and rewarding yourself along the way.

5. Stay disciplined - Remember that achieving financial success takes discipline and perseverance. Stay focused on your goals and don't let setbacks derail you.

"IN SUMMARY, TAKING CONTROL OF YOUR FINANCES REQUIRES ACTION, DISCIPLINE, AND PERSEVERANCE. YOU HAVE THE KNOWLEDGE AND TOOLS TO ACHIEVE FINANCIAL SUCCESS - NOW IT'S UP TO YOU TO TAKE THE FIRST STEP."

REMEMBER, EVERY SMALL ACTION YOU TAKE IS A STEP TOWARDS A BRIGHTER FINANCIAL FUTURE. SO GO AHEAD AND TAKE THAT FIRST STEP TODAY!

Final Thoughts and Resources for Further Learning

Congratulations again on taking the first step towards mastering your personal finances! As you continue on your financial journey, here are some final thoughts and resources to help you along the way.

First, remember that financial success is not a one-time event - it's a lifelong journey. Keep educating yourself, setting new goals, and taking action to achieve them.

Second, don't be afraid to seek out help when you need it. There are many resources available, including financial advisors, credit counselling services, and online communities where you can connect with others who are on a similar journey.

Finally, here are some recommended resources for further learning:

Personal finance blogs - There are many personal finance blogs that offer great advice and insights on managing your money. Some popular ones include The Penny Hoarder, Frugalwoods, and Mr. Money Mustache.

Books - There are countless books on personal finance, investing, and wealth building. Some classic titles include "The Total Money Makeover" by Dave Ramsey, "The Millionaire Next Door" by Thomas J. Stanley and William D. Danko, and "The Intelligent Investor" by Benjamin Graham.

Online courses - There are many online courses available on personal finance and investing. Some popular ones include "Personal Finance 101" on Udemy, "The Investing Blueprint" on Skillshare, and "Financial Literacy Bootcamp" on Coursera.

"REMEMBER, FINANCIAL SUCCESS IS WITHIN YOUR REACH - IT JUST TAKES KNOWLEDGE, PLANNING, AND ACTION. KEEP LEARNING, STAY FOCUSED ON YOUR GOALS, AND NEVER GIVE UP!"